D0734517

heart

These quotations were gathered lovingly but unscientifically over several years and/or contributed by many friends or acquaintances. Some arrived, and survived in our files, on scraps of paper and may therefore be imperfectly worded or attributed. To the authors, contributors and original sources, our thanks, and where appropriate, our apologies.—The editors

C R E D I T S

Compiled by Kobi Yamada

Designed by Steve Potter

ISBN: 1-888387-63-7

Printed in China

The heart can do anything.

MOLIERE

Down deep in every human soul is a hidden long- ing, impulse, and ambition to do something fine and enduring.

GRENVILLE KLEISER

THERE IS IN US SOMETHING WISER
THAN OUR HEAD.

SCHOPENHAUER

Knowledge

is dangerous

unless it goes

through

the heart.

CELTIC SAYING

It seems to me we can never give up longing and wishing while we are thoroughly alive. There are certain things we feel to be beautiful and good, and we must hunger after them.

GEORGE ELIOT

Only passions,

great passions,

can elevate

the soul to

great things.

DENIS DIDEROT

IF YOU

DON'T KNOW WHAT YOUR PASSION IS, REALIZE THAT ONE REASON FOR YOUR EXISTENCE ON EARTH

IS TO FIND IT.

OPRAH WINFREY

Let yourself
be silently
drawn
by the
strange
pull of what
you really
love.

RUMI

WHERESOEVER YOU GO,
GO WITH ALL YOUR HEART.

CONFUCIUS

The minute you begin

to do what you really

want to do, it's really

a different kind of life.

BUCKMINSTER FULLER

FOLLOW YOUR DESIRE AS LONG AS YOU LIVE.

P T A H - H O T E P

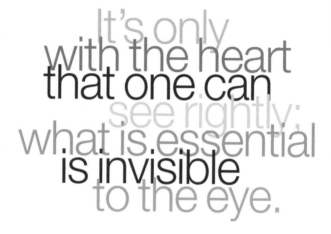

It's only
with the heart
that one can
see rightly;
what is essential
is invisible
to the eye.

ANTOINE DE SAINT-EXUPERY

Where your pleasure is,

there is your treasure;

where your treasure,

there your heart;

where your heart,

there your happiness.

AUGUSTINE

I think people don't

place a high enough value

on how much they

are nurtured by doing

whatever it is that

totally absorbs them.

JEAN SHINODA BOLEN, M.D.

NOW FOR SOME HEART WORK.

RAINER MARIA RILKE

There are many things in life that will catch your eye, but only a few will catch your heart. Pursue these.

MICHAEL NOLAN

No one else
can tell you what
    your life's work is,
but it's important
    that you find it.
There is a part of you
that knows—
    affirm that part.

WILLIS W. HARMAN

TAKE YOUR HEART TO WORK

AND ASK THE MOST AND BEST

OF YOURSELF AND EVERYBODY

ELSE. DON'T LET YOUR SPECIAL

CHARACTER AND SPIRIT—THE

TRUE ESSENCE OF YOU—DON'T

LET THAT GET BEATEN DOWN.

MERYL STREEP

When you

believe in something,

and you carry it

in your heart,

you accept no excuses,

only results.

KEN BLANCHARD

What matters in today's world is not the difference between those who believe and those who do not believe, but the difference between those who care and those who don't.

ABBE PIRE

Your work is a mirror image of yourself and the company you work for. What shows on the outside is a good indication of what is taking place on the inside.

CHARLOTTE ELICH

The outward work can never be small if the inward one is great, and the outward work can never be great if the inward is small or of little worth. There is your life and there alone you live and your work lives.

MEISTER ECKHART

Quality is not just
a chart, or a standard,
or a specification—
it's a state of mind,
a commitment,
a responsibility, a spirit.
It's a way of doing,
being and living.

DON GALER

BY THE WORK ONE KNOWS THE WORKMAN.

JEAN DE LA FONTAINE

The only thing that makes one place more attractive to me than another is the quantity of heart I find in it.

JANE WELSH CARLYLE

People don't care

how much you know

until they know

how much you care.

MIKE MCNIGHT

If I can relate to this moment with integrity, and then this moment with integrity, and then this moment with integrity, then the sum of that is going to be great over a lifetime.

JON KABAT-ZINN, PH.D.

Whoever I am

or whatever

I am doing,

some kind of

excellence is within

my reach.

JOHN GARDNER

HEART, INSTINCT, PRINCIPLES.

BLAISE PASCAL

CARING
IS EVERYTHING.

BARON FRIEDRICH VON HUGEL

In every community,
there is work
to be done.
In every nation,
there are wounds
to heal.
In every heart,
there is the
power to do it.

MARIANNE WILLIAMSON

THE GREATEST TRAGEDY IS
INDIFFERENCE.

THE RED CROSS

The opposite
of love is not hate,
it's indifference…
And the opposite
of life
is not death,
it's indifference.

ELIE WIESEL

God calls you to

the place where

your deep gladness

and the world's

deep hunger meet.

FREDERICK BUECHNER

Imagine what a harmonious world it could be if every single person, both young and old, share a little of what he or she is good at doing.

QUINCY JONES

PERSON
TO PERSON,
MOMENT
TO MOMENT,
AS WE LOVE,
WE CHANGE
THE WORLD.

SAMAHRIA LYTE KAUFMAN

There is no feeling
in a human heart
which exists in
that heart alone—
which is not, in some
form or degree,
in every heart.

GEORGE MACDONALD

Give of
your hands
to serve
and your
hearts
to love.

MOTHER TERESA

THE SALVATION OF THE WORLD LIES IN
THE HUMAN HEART.

V A C L A V   H A V E L

Love is the

key to life, and

its influences

are those that

move the world.

RALPH TRINE

A GOOD HEAD AND A GOOD HEART
ARE ALWAYS A FORMIDABLE COMBINATION.

NELSON MANDELA

When you are
no longer compelled
by desire or fear—
when you simply
follow your bliss—
doors will open
where you would
not have thought
there were doors—
and the world will
step in and help.

JOSEPH CAMPBELL

Seek out that
particular mental attribute
which makes you
feel most deeply and
vitally alive, along with
which comes the
inner voice which says,
'this is the real me',
and when you have
found that attitude,
follow it.

WILLIAM JAMES

IT'S ABOUT FOLLOWING YOUR BLISS,
    LOSING IT, AND FINDING IT AGAIN.

NATALIE CHAPMAN

Everyone should carefully observe which way his heart draws him, and then choose that way with all his strength.

HASIDIC SAYING

There are many wonderful things that will never be done if you do not do them.

HONORABLE CHARLES D. GILL

The mind

determines

what's possible.

The heart

surpasses it.

PILAR COOLINTA

NEVER CUT LOOSE FROM YOUR LONGINGS.

AMOS OZ

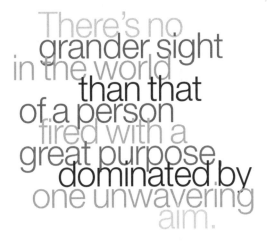

There's no grander sight in the world than that of a person fired with a great purpose, dominated by one unwavering aim.

ORISON SWETT MARDEN

DO THE KINDS OF THINGS

THAT COME FROM THE HEART.

WHEN YOU DO, YOU WON'T

BE DISSATISFIED, YOU WON'T

BE ENVIOUS, YOU WON'T BE

LONGING FOR SOMEBODY ELSE'S

THINGS. ON THE CONTRARY,

YOU'LL BE OVERWHELMED

WITH WHAT COMES BACK.

MORRIE SCHWARTZ

Strong lives
are motivated
by dynamic
purpose.

HILDEBRAND KENNET

I never achieved great fame—no heights of incredible glory. But I think that any strong endeavor that gives you a sense of joy is the greatest thing in life.

SONO OSATO

THE KIND OF BEAUTY

I WANT MOST IS

THE HARD-TO-GET KIND

THAT COMES

FROM WITHIN—

STRENGTH, COURAGE,

DIGNITY.

RUBY DEE

THE THINGS
THAT MATTER THE MOST
IN THIS WORLD,
THEY CAN NEVER
BE HELD
IN OUR HAND.

GLORIA GAITHER

Whatever else we may do with the time of our lives, nothing can be of more enduring consequence than the hours we give to the health and growth of our own hearts.

ROBERT SEXTON

WE MUST NOT ONLY EDUCATE THE MIND,
BUT ALSO THE HEART.

KOBI YAMADA

The biggest

thing in the world,

bigger than the

ocean and the sky,

is your heart.

D. H.   C H O E

the good life™

Celebrating the joy of living fully.

Also available are these spirited companion books in The Good Life series of great quotations:

yes!
refresh
moxie
hero
friend
spirit
success
joy
thanks